A GUIDE
TO LONDON'S
CLASSIC
CAFES

and

FISH &
CHIP
SHOPS

**black dog
publishing**
london uk

SPECIALS OF THE DAY

PROLOGUE
Phoebe Stubbs   4

INTRODUCTION
Simon Majumdar   6

CENTRAL LONDON
Bar Italia   12
City Snacks   16
Diana's Diner   18
Golden Union *   20
North Sea Fish Restaurant *   24
Porky's Pantry   28
Rock & Sole Plaice *   30
Sorrento Snack Bar   32
The Fryer's Delight *   34
Valtaro Snack bar   38

NORTH LONDON
Double Six Cafe   42
Ellie's   44
Nautilus *   46
Poseidon *   48
Rheidol Rooms   50
Sea Shell of Lisson Grove *   54
Toff's of Muswell Hill *   58
Two Brothers *   60

SOUTH LONDON
Brady's Fish Restaurant *   64
Fish Club *   66
Gambardella   68
Masters Super Fish *   72
Maries Cafe   74
My Tea Shop   78
Olley's *   80
Regency Cafe   84
Something Fishy *   88
Terry's   90
The Flying Fish *   94
The Phoenix   96
The Sea Cow *   100
Tony's Café   104
Tony's   108

FISH OF THE DAY

EAST LONDON

Arthur's Café	112
Beppe's Café	116
Cafe Bliss	118
City Corner	122
E. Pellicci	124
Faulkners *	128
Fish House *	130
L. Rodi	132
Luis' Café	136
Poppies *	138
Scotti's Snack Bar	142
The Regis Snack Bar	146
The Shepherdess	148

WEST LONDON

Blandford's	152
Frank's Sandwich Bar	154
Gino's Cappuccino Bar	156
Geales Fish Restaurant *	158
George's Portobello Fish Bar *	160
Hickey's Cafe Rest	162
Kerbisher & Malt *	166
Raffles Cafe Diner	170

GLOSSARY	172
AUTHOR BIOGRAPHY	174
IMAGE CREDITS	174
THANKS	174

*Fish & Chip Shop

PROLOGUE

It is hard to define those features that lend a cafe or fish &
chip shop its classic status. It's not just the food—the breakfast
fry-ups, meat pudding, cod and chips or pie and mash we often
hope for from these places—though if a classic cafe were to
solely serve contemporary dishes, it would likely get struck off
this list. The same would be the case if the fish & chips on offer
weren't, in our opinion, of the best there is in the city. The word
'classic' does not define a certain decade; there are cafes and
restaurants in this book whose decorative features hail from the
1920s up to the present, and many have a mismatching mix of
all the decades in between. Rather, our best description, and
therefore criteria for inclusion in this book, is that with these
things combined, there is a feeling you get on entering and being
accepted that warms the soul. This is therefore a group of cafes
and restaurants that epitomise this openness and this particular
warmth of one of our treasured London food traditions.

For classic cafe and fish & chip shop aficionados, you will find
in these pages many classic WM Still and Son tea and coffee
makers to ogle over, much formica and worn, faded booth
seating to swallow your time in, but the cafes and restaurants
in the following pages are more than the sum of their features;
they stand, on the most part, on years of tradition. They are often
family run, independent bastions of ordinary food for all people
in the capital. Their food is not 'on trend' or 'gastro' fare for the
foodie. Rather, it is hearty, designed to sustain the worker for
the day. These cafes and chippies are mostly place-specific and
local—part of the scenery, so much so you might have to read
this to remember that they are right on your doorstep. Both
fish & chip shops and classic cafes have in common a certain

'Britishness', a feeling of homeliness, even a steadfast sameness that makes one feel as though anyone could walk in and always feel welcome. That is, they are something akin to a genuine American diner, 'greasy spoon' or the simple, but ever more cherished, 'Mom and Pop' restaurants one can still just find in any number of countries around the world. And while these are seemingly on the wane, it is this specialness that we celebrate here.

Where traditional food is concerned we have noticed that where what we want from our classic cafes has to do with the past, with nostalgia and localness, what we want from our fish & chip shop has evolved. Fish restaurants are steadily becoming more gentrified and we have included those who have done this successfully. Notable examples are Brady's and Golden Union, which are here because they exemplify a respect for the cafes and fish & chip restaurants of old, but feel contemporary in styling and serve fresh, sustainable fish under sound ethical policies.

This guide is intended as a glimpse into a part of London that we often overlook. Divided into five areas—Central, North, South, East and West—wherever you live or stay, you will find a hearty meal at a reasonable price nearby, served in notable surroundings full of history and character.

Phoebe Stubbs

INTRODUCTION

If, as I have, you were to write a book about the history of British food, you would soon find that you used two words more than most others. Those words would be "immigration" and "trade". Without these factors, the cuisine of this sceptred isle would be missing some of its most famous dishes; including clotted cream, kippers, the gin and tonic and, of course, our national dish, the chicken tikka masala.

Nowhere is British food's dependence on immigration more apparent than when one discusses two of its most familiar landmarks, fish & chip shops and cafes or "Caffs" as they might more rightly be called. Both of these honorable institutions owe their presence in no small part to the fact that Britain has traded with other nations since before written records and that we have always been an immensely tolerant country who, for centuries, have been willing to accept political and religious refugees from all over the globe. These migrants and merchants brought with them their own culinary traditions which over time fused with those of other communities already living in Britain to produce new and often wonderful results.

The arrival of fish & chips was a happy culinary accident caused by the arrival of the Marrano, Sephardic Jews from Portugal in the seventeenth century, who brought with them considerable skills in fish frying, and fleeing Belgians who knew a thing or three about how to fry a potato. Both dishes soon became established as street food options in their own right and there is even record of Thomas Jefferson making reference to sampling "Fish fried in the Jewish fashion" while in London during the latter part of the eighteenth century.

While there is a heated debate about where the two ingredients were first combined into the nation's meal of choice, I favour the claim of Joseph Malin who, in 1860 opened a shop selling fried fish with chipped potatoes in Whitechapel, London, not only giving himself a fond place in the fatty heart of every Briton, but also cementing the capital's claim to be the spiritual home of fish and chips.

It is hard to overestimate the importance of the fish & chip shop in British culture since then. By the beginning of the twentieth century there were over 25,000 shops nationwide and it was one of the few foods that escaped the grim horror of rationing during the Second World War, so important did the government believe the dish to be to the nation's morale.

Their numbers may now have dwindled to less than half that figure, but the glow of a great 'chippie' is still one of the most welcoming sights on any frosty night when only fried food is good for what ails you.

By comparison to the fish & chip shop, the cafe may seem to be a more recent arrival on our high streets, but they too have long roots going back to the opening of the first coffee houses in London and Oxford in the middle of the seventeenth century when merchants first began selling this black liquid to a curious public. By the early stages of the nineteenth century, these coffee houses had taken on the name 'café', from the French for Coffee House and had become firmly entrenched as a favourite meeting place for London's intellectual elite.

Their popularity continued, with some ups and downs until the end of the Second World War, when there was a rapid growth in the number of cafes in London with the mass arrival of families from Italy, many of whom were joining Italian prisoners of war who had chosen to remain in Britain when fighting ceased.

As Britain began to rediscover its confidence after years of conflict and rationing, so too did cafe culture begin to boom, not only with young people who used the cafes and 'milk bars' as places to congregate and listen to the latest imported records from America, but also with working people who knew they could depend on their local 'greasy spoon' for a dependable meal at a good price.

Although the "Full English" breakfast actually owes its existence to the boom in numbers of UK bed and breakfast hotels during the 1950s and 1960s, it soon became the cafes to which the hungover would turn when eggs, bacon, sausages, fried bread, mushrooms, black pudding, beans, toast and builder's tea seemed like the only cure to the excesses of the night before.

From the early 1980s onwards, however, the numbers of traditional cafes, like those of fish & chip shops, began to decline. The upwardly mobile nature of immigrant families meant that the children of the original owners had little intention of finding themselves behind the counter once they had finished their hard won education, while the costs of food and rent began to spiral to a point where it was impossible to make a living. Add to that the explosion of new dining options and the public's unquenchable search for the latest trend, and both of these stalwarts of the UK scene looked like they might receive a permanent place on the endangered species list until they simply died away altogether. Thankfully, the story of the fish & chip shop and the humble cafe is not yet at an end; in more recent years they have both undergone something of a revival as British food has rightfully begun to stand up for itself in the ranks of world cuisine and as young chefs and entrepreneurs have given a fresh and appealing modern overhaul to both menus and decor. At the same time many of the existing cafes and 'chippies' are finally being recognised—and even protected—for what they are, national treasures.

All of which means that the readers of this guide have a unique opportunity to eat a true slice (or should that be fried slice?) of British history by visiting examples, both modern and historical of places that fed a nation in both its good and its darkest times. So make full use of them, enjoy your meals and wherever you end up have a large cup of builder's tea for me.

Simon Majumdar

Bar Italia

CENTRAL LONDON

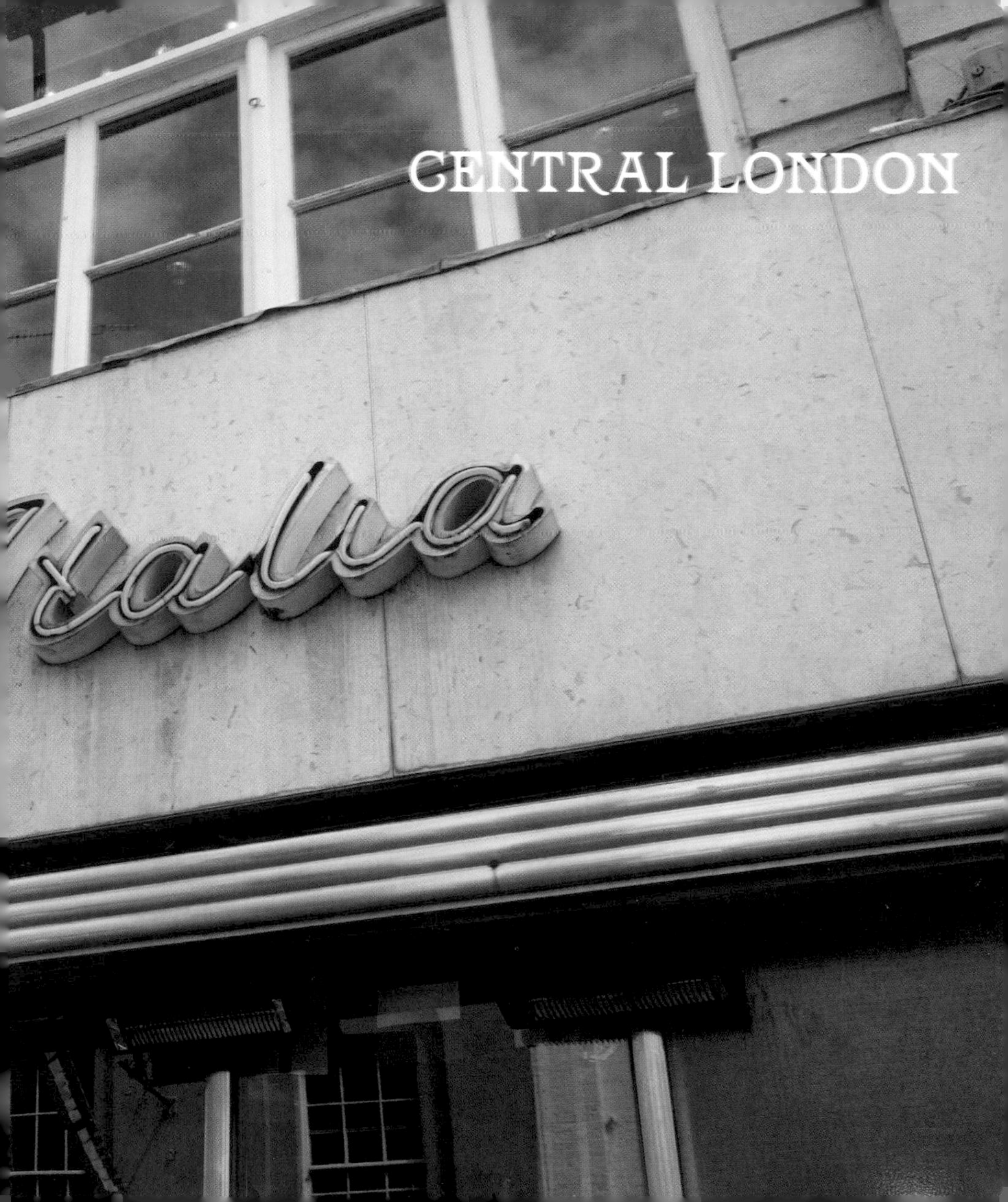

BAR ITALIA

This renowned Italian cafe was founded in 1949 by Lou and Caterina Polledri, grandparents of the current owners, Antonio, Luigi and Veronica. Catering runs deep in their family and the current generation of owners is proud to continue in its grandparents' footsteps.

When the cafe first opened it had the important role of providing not just good coffee to Londoners but a social centre for the Italian community in London at the time. The jubilant crowds around the place during Italian football matches are testament to the lasting success of this aim. But Italian or not, all are welcome here for coffee and snacks at all times of the day. The coffees are a hugely important part of what makes this cafe great. Proper cappuccinos are served strong, with a delicate and deep foam on top and their espressos will kick start anyone's day. They also have a mouth-watering selection of cakes and treats under the glass counter and offer freshly squeezed juices, sandwiches and iced blended drinks too.

For the owners, it has been important to keep the classic cafe feel. Many original pieces of the bar remain from 1949. Their Gaggia coffee machine has been making great coffee for 50 years now. Italian ephemera is squeezed into every available space, transporting you instantly out of busy Soho into another world—a family-run cafe founded on the principles of community, serving good coffee in a great atmosphere.

Address

22 Frith Street
Soho
W1D 4RP

Telephone

020 7437 4520

CITY SNACKS

It is a well-know London fact that cab drivers know this city better than anyone else; from the best back routes to the cheapest pubs to the most reliably good cafes, a cab driver will know the answer. It is a good sign, then, that City Snacks, on Theobald's Road just opposite trendy and rather beautiful Lamb's Conduit Street, is full of cab drivers on their break.

The perspex sign above the door tells you immediately that it's a classic. The retro 'C' merging into an 'S' graphic next to the words "City Snacks", no doubt designed in the cafe's 1980s heyday is now looking quite on-trend again. Inside it is packed with Italian treats, mugs, posters and trinkets either side of the two rows of small booths. The tables, probably once red but now reddish orangey, more from being well-loved and over-used than seeing the sun in this narrow cafe, are all situated well past the busy bar area towards the back. The sausages, though really quite tasty, are not the certified organic variety and it is unlikely that the eggs are either, but for a sausage and egg sandwich in a crusty roll slathered with butter at only £2.50, that's well worth overlooking. Coupled with a cup of builder's tea, you would be ready to handle the bizarre contents of the nearby Sir John Soane's Museum, a Georgian house-sized cabinet of curiosities on the north side of Lincoln's Inn Fields.

Address

29 Theobald's Road
WC1X 8SP

Bloomsbury

DIANA'S DINER

Address

39 Endell Street
Covent Garden
WC2H 9BA

Telephone

020 7240 0272

Right bang in the centre of Covent Garden (well, off Long Acre on Endell Street, in fairly close proximity to Rock & Sole Plaice), this restaurant has become a favourite with tourists who are not thrilled at the astronomical prices of their £15 hotel fry-ups. You can get a reliable breakfast at Diana's for around £5. And if you are lucky, you might see a celebrity, as stars are spotted here on a regular basis. The cafe even features in a wacky story involving Jon Marsh of the band The Beloved. He placed an advert reading "I am Jon Marsh, founder of The Beloved. Should you too wish to do something gorgeous, meet me in three year's time at Diana's Diner, or site thereof, Covent Garden, London, WC2"; given that this was written in 1983, "site thereof" has been proved to be utterly unnecessary, such is the longevity of this place.

The current owner began as a dishwasher over two decades ago and then gradually took on more responsibility until taking over the lease 15 years ago. It is hard to keep the prices as low as he would like. With rising rents, Covent Garden is not an easy area in which to have a small cafe that can cater to those on a tight budget.

The cafe serves a huge array of food, given its size. Home-made pies go down well, as do the fish & chips. A Full English and a cup of tea comes to under £6, but you can get "The Special" with black pudding and 'bubble' for a little more and enjoy it amid the faces and autographs of those celebrities who have eaten here during their time on the West End stage.

GOLDEN UNION

Golden Union is a popular spot. In the decor the owners wanted to invoke a classic fish & chip shop like those they remembered from childhood. Its location in bustling Soho, Golden Union means it manages to be both a place that draws on childhood memories of classic styling and combines a more modern take on a chippy. The interior is clean and contemporary yet still retro, not too removed from a classic cafe and chip shop interior, complete with pickles behind the fryers, but brought up to date—a large neon Golden Union sign at the back completes the look against Tube station-style tiling and formica table tops.

As the restaurant is fully licensed, you can enjoy your freshly cooked fish & chips or pie with a beer or a glass of wine. Given its location just off Oxford Street at the top of Poland Street, this is a blessing for a tired shopper. Golden Union serves a large cod for £7.15 and a small for £5.65, coupled with chips this is not the cheapest fish & chips in the area but, given the quality and dedication to freshness (chips are hand-cut every day), it is considered one of the best. There is also a specific board for the daily delivered fresh fish, featuring items such as rock salmon, pollock, coley and prawns, among others. For those on the go, Golden Union do takeaways in probably the smartest takeaway fish containers in London—a handy way to munch as you take in the sights of Soho.

Address

38 Poland Street
Soho
W1F 7LY

Telephone

020 7434 1933

Website

goldenunion.co.uk

NORTH SEA FISH RESTAURANT

Address

7–8 Leigh St
Bloomsbury
WC1H 9EW

Telephone

020 7388 9770

Set in a quiet street in Bloomsbury, the inside of this restaurant is comfortingly traditional, unlikely to have changed since it was founded. The bar is well-stocked with Scotch; wooden beams and red carpet cocoon the diner in a retro haven of formal 1970s; and diners eat off mats that inform about the many varieties of fish on offer. The restaurant has a steady stream of elderly locals who have been eating here for years. However, it is not unusual to hear an American accent, as many tourists come here to experience classic fish & chips at its best. And they are rarely disappointed. The batter is extremely light and crispy, the chips are seldom soggy, tending on the crispy side with fluffy centres.

The restaurant has a small takeaway next door where it is possible to get fish & chips for around half the price of the restaurant, though up to the same exacting standards. At lunchtimes they offer a small portion of either cod or haddock and chips for only £3.50. On a nice day we recommend getting a takeaway fish & chips and going across the street to a small park where there are a number of unusual benches in the shape of animals. With a small playground, it is just the thing to do for parents eating with children. For those who don't like fish, the restaurant has a number of other dishes, such as steak and chips, and the takeaway does a good trade in chicken, pies and battered sausages. But the main attraction is undoubtedly the fish. The jumbo portion can easily be shared between two and offers excellent value for money.

TRY OUR MINI
PORTION of
Fish and Chips
£3.50

Plaice

Plie • Passera di mare • Platija • Scholle • Solha
高眼鲽 • Rødspette • アカガレイ • камбала

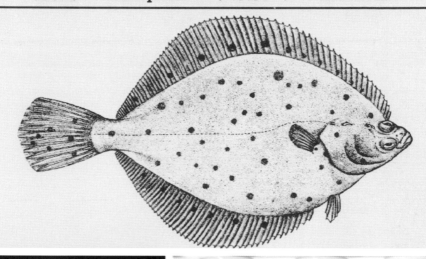

Specials

Dover Sole	£14.25
Lemon Sole	£11.95
Scotch Salmon	£10.45
Rainbow Trout	£7.95
Plaice on the Bone	£8.95
Halibut Steak	£11.75
Scotch Scampi	£6.45
Seafood Platter	£7.45

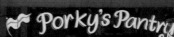

PORKY'S PANTRY

Porky's Pantry is a small cafe tucked in to Chandos Place, only a short walk from Covent Garden. As its name suggests it has a 'piggy' theme and the interior is peppered with little ceramic pig figurines, porcine calendars and other porky ephemera.

Porky's gets very busy at lunchtimes, with their small seating area of only two two-seater booths and four four-seater booths filling up quickly with regulars, particularly between mid-day and 2 pm. Space is tight but it is all well-used. And despite the crowds, Mark, the owner, will make you feel welcome.

The sandwiches at Porky's Pantry are popular with the local work crowd, who regularly queue onto the street to get their takeaways. If you go here for a sit-down meal it is well worth having dessert, known here as "afters"—large potions of apple pie, cherry pie or bread pudding, all served with custard and ice-cream. However, making room for these will be tricky after the large portions of their main courses, which only cost between £5.40 and £6.80 and feature well-loved favourites such as omelettes, steak and kidney and mushroom pie, chilli con carne and fish & chips.

Address

49 Chandos Place
Covent Garden
WC2N 4HS

Telephone

020 7836 0967

ROCK & SOLE PLAICE

As the oldest surviving fish & chip shop in London, Rock & Sole Plaice is clearly getting something right. Established in 1871, the restaurant still serves mainly fish classics such as cod or haddock and chips, but also has a number of other dishes, all of which only serve to reiterate its classic status: steak and kidney pies, Cornish pasties, plaice, onion rings and Heinz baked beans, among many others.

The staff are incredibly friendly and make you feel at home, and food comes out really quickly. Prices are what you would expect for this part of town but portions are enormous. We ate a huge cod with chips, which are themselves more like the size you would expect from roast potatoes, and a vast haddock and chips and a large salad. All were delicious. The fish's batter was thin, dark and audibly crispy, and the chips were pale yet the perfect combination of crisp and soft.

Upstairs the decor is fitting for a fish & chip shop of its age—white tiles painted with signage in cursive script—and outside a large section of tables are covered from the sun (or rain) with large umbrellas. There is further seating downstairs, and to head down there is to descend under the brightest of seas. The room, which seats around 30, is painted with an underwater mural of 'friendly' sea creatures complete with the hull of a small boat—a sight that could cheer up even the weariest tourist on a damp London day.

Address

47 Endell Street
Covent Garden
WC2H 9AJ

Telephone

020 7836 3785

SORRENTO SNACK BAR

Address

8 Woburn Walk
Bloomsbury
WC1H 0JL

Telephone

020 7388 3554

Sorrento Snack Bar is set on a quiet, charmingly 'Dickensian' street in historic Bloomsbury, providing sustenance to passers-by on a tight budget. Not a greasy spoon, but a classic little snack bar with a beautiful and traditional frontage in a convenient location for catching a train at Euston, which is less than five minutes away. When we were there the sun was shining and people were chatting over cups of tea at tables in the pedestrianised and tree-lined Woburn Walk. Locals all seem to be known by name to the team of ladies who run the place, and endearingly call everybody else "darling".

If you arrive at the start of the day, perhaps after a ride on the last remaining sleeper train in the UK from Scotland to Euston, the breakfast you will get here is decidedly traditional. You can specify how you would like your eggs cooked and they even freshly poach eggs for the more health-conscious among their visitors. If a cooked breakfast is not your cup of tea, they also have a range of other meals available, notably their own home-made cakes and biscuits and, for lunch, Italian classics such as lasagne, a daily risotto and home-made soup.

Their classic fixed-seat interior of only four tables doesn't easily accommodate those of a larger build, but the decent coffee at more than reasonable prices makes it worth standing or perching on one of the bar stools.

THE FRYER'S DELIGHT

The outside of The Fryer's Delight clues the diner in to the experience they might have inside. The sign is a classic—a happy big-mouthed cod doffing his bowler hat and proclaiming "the tastiest fish & chips in town", and customers will not be disappointed with what they are served here.

Known for its period interior as much as its food, The Fryer's Delight is a treasured London gem. The interior colour scheme immediately dates the place to its founding in 1962: bright orange and blue formica gleam in the dangling overhead lights which are reflected in the shiny dropped ceiling panels. The bar is covered with the usual chippy accoutrements—pickled eggs, gherkins and sauces.

The fish here is good. This is the place to go if you like your batter thick and stodgy, but it is really the chips that steal the show. Cooked in beef dripping until crispy and delicious, these are not for the pescatarian. Though at £1.50 for a huge portion, they are a very good deal. There is only one table with two chairs on Theobald's Road, but it is well worth sitting here to admire the exterior signage; a sea of blue and white mosaic tiles sit under the window, against which variations on the 'best fish & chips in town' signs are repeated.

Address

19 Theobald's Road
Bloomsbury
WC1X 8SL

Telephone

020 7405 4114

THE FRYER'S DELIGHT
for the Tastiest Fish & Chips in town

Fresh-Pack Pickles
TRADITIONAL CHIP SHOP
PICKLED ONIONS

PICKLED EGGS

THE
FRYER'S DELIGHT
19 THEOBALD'S RD. HOLBORN, W.C.1

SEA-FRESH FISH &
HOME-GROWN POTATOES

TELEPHONE
405-4114

FISH & CHIPS

CONSIDERED BY
MANY THE
FINEST
IN LONDON

Salmon Pasta	POLLO PASTA	NAPOLI PASTA	Chicken Pesto Pasta
salmon in creamy pinky sauce	(Chicken bacon mushroon)	(Tomato sauce)	Chicken in pesto creamy white sauce
£4.30	£4.30	£3.30	£4.30

VALTARO
SNACK BAR

Valtaro Snack Bar is a tiny place with no tables, only a line of counters and stools around its periphery, perched on which you will mostly find either local workmen or students, depending on the time of day. You can't miss the bright turquoise awning outside, even if it obscures the cafe's name. We entered following an elderly gentleman who sat down in what appeared to be 'his' corner. The exchange that followed perfectly summed up the establishment: "Usual?", "Usual", after which his lunch was brought out immediately.

The kitchen area is tiny, but the staff manage to churn out huge portions of freshly cooked pasta for hungover students with ease and at an incredibly low price; most range between £3 and £4. We had a large spaghetti bolognese which was only £3.50 and came covered with Parmesan cheese, albeit the packet variety. These pasta dishes and the large cooked breakfasts are the cafe's mainstay, but it also has on its specials menu of scattered A4 sheets of paper a few British 'classics' as well—liver and onions, corned beef and mushrooms on toast amongst them. The rest of the menu consists of standard snack bar fare: omelettes and chips, sandwiches with a staggering selection of fillings and hearty jacket potatoes.

On warmer days you can sit outside at little tables on the street, soaking up the atmosphere of this pleasant and surprisingly quiet part of town.

Address

88 Marchmont Street
Bloomsbury
WC1N 1AG

Telephone

020 7388 5829

Rheidol Rooms

NORTH LONDON

DOUBLE SIX CAFE

Address

66 Eversholt Street
King's Cross
NW1 1DA

Telephone

020 7388 5829

London's Euston Road is an inhospitable first sight for the many tourists who come in to Euston, St Pancras or King's Cross along its northern side. The two lanes of traffic are noisy, fast and have no patience for pedestrians. What few eateries exist are of the chain variety and the shops are largely convenience stores or internet cafes with extortionate prices. It will be a relief, therefore, to take a left out of Euston down Eversholt Street to find this small, often packed cafe. It isn't 'special' but rather its charm is in its ordinariness.

The interior isn't sure whether it is still a classic or not. There are green leatherette booths and formica tables and the small front opens out to a larger, brighter back area which at 10.30 am was full of local construction workers on a break. There is a brand new coffee machine and bar at the front, meaning that the decor hovers somewhere between classic cafe and contemporary coffee shop.

The waitress withstood some of the clientele's chauvinist banter with a well-fixed smile, managing to remain steadfastly pleasant to everyone, despite the comments. Breakfast was reliably good and cheap. Two poached eggs on toast, scrambled eggs on toast with bacon and two teas came to a little over £7. Lunch is a classic affair—braised lamb boilpot with two veg; ham, eggs and chips; egg salad; and sausage and chips all feature.

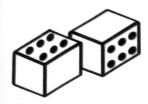

ELLIE'S

Well known as a good spot for a hangover cure, Ellie's is well loved by locals in the Brondesbury area, just a short walk from Kilburn station. The walls are an unusually bright shade of purple against the more classic wooden furniture. Down the road is a specialist music school and there is, as it happens, an enthusiastic rock music theme in the decor, set up to lure the students; during the school year, it will be hard to find a table at lunch time —students with their valuable instruments come here for the varied menu that has adapted to suit the new clientele and changing population. More health-aware elements such as salads and paninis, Mediterranean dishes and halloumi now co-habit with the classic breakfasts and shepherds pies. For those less inclined towards salad or vegetables, a Full English is served for only £4.80. However, for a breakfast with a twist try Ellie's Special Breakfast: garlic salami, hash browns, feta filo pastry, a fried egg, mushrooms and tomato.

The new influx of students has not altered the cafe completely. Breakfast is still served all day to local workers who happily share the space with the students, often reading the paper or looking out of the window, and they also do a good trade in teas in the afternoon. There's no fuss here; Coca-Cola is served in its can with the addition of a straw if you want it.

Address

316 Kilburn High Road
Brondesbury
NW6 2DG

Telephone

020 7328 7327

NAUTILUS

Address

27–29 Fortune Green Road
West Hampstead
NW6 1DU

Telephone

020 7435 2532

Nautilus has been a family-run business ever since it opened in 1948. A long time has passed since the good old newsprint wrapping days, but the quality of the fish handled at Nautilus has remained consistently high. Bought every day from Billingsgate, cod, haddock, and other familiar fish are lovingly cut and freshly fried in matzo meal. A classic Kosher establishment catering for Hampstead's Jewish community, it is considered the place to go for fish in the area. Many tourists make their way here too; attracted by word-of-mouth recommendation, they choose Nautilus for their inaugural chippy experience.

Connie has been in charge of both chippy and restaurant ever since the previous Greek owners retired. The place has stayed the same; wooden panelling and rustic chairs in the restaurant welcome locals who attend regularly to have grilled Dover sole and plaice on the bone. A short but well formed wine list has been selected by Connie herself to complement the fish dishes.

If the more pricey sit-in option does not attract you, Fortune Green opposite the shop, as well as nearby Hampstead Heath, provide unrivalled scenery to enjoy your takeaway meal. Cod and chips will cost you £7.80, and beware, portions are big!

Nautilus
FISH RESTAURANT

POSEIDON

Poseidon has always been a popular East Finchley chippy, that owners Stelios and Stefano enlarged by acquiring the space next door and adding a sit-down restaurant in 2003. The space allowed them to expand on their name's mythological theme: Poseidon restaurant combines neat and simple furniture with a wall covered by a painting representing the Greek god of the sea at work. There is even a reference book on the Greek deities available at the counter, for the incurably curious.

A selection of Greek starters, such as taramasalata, olives and feta cheese feature alongside the more purely oceanic options, such as octopus, squid and oysters. Their signature fresh fish, which here is covered in matzo flour if desired and fried in groundnut oil or grilled as a healthy alternative, features classic cod, haddock and skate together with more unusual catches, such as swordfish and turbot. There are plenty of home-made desserts available—pineapple caramel cake, rice pudding—as well as those sorbet-filled giant lemons that feature in the set menus of all worthy fish restaurants of the Mediterranean.

Poseidon has been a classic of many a local fish suppers, with regulars often driving there to get their takeaway cod—still for only £6.50—despite having moved further afield. Sticking around the area is also an interesting option: the beautiful Phoenix Cinema, one of UK's oldest purpose-built operating cinemas, is just a couple of blocks away. A great way to spend a quiet evening after your fishy feast.

Address

102 High Road
East Finchley
N2 9EB

Telephone

020 8883 5296

RHEIDOL ROOMS

Address

16 Rheidol Terrace
Islington
N1 8NS

Telephone

020 7226 8674

The Rheidol Rooms is the last remaining classic cafe in upmarket Islington. It is not tatty or worn, but rather a beautifully preserved classic with owners who know how special the place is and look after it accordingly.

The exterior has been smartly painted olive green, framing the huge windows which light up the bright interior on even the dullest London day. Regulars sit at 'their' tables and chat to each other while their food is prepared in the well-organised kitchen at the back. All the food is fresh and home-made. We had a delicious daily special of shepherd's pie with cabbage and potatoes, which was huge for its £4.60 price and came with thick, hot gravy in a gravy boat. We were then tempted into dessert by the sight of a jam roll which came out steaming and doused in custard to our neighbour's table. Ours, at only £1.60, was the most delicious and best value dessert we had eaten in a long time—the kind of pudding that transports one back to holidays by the seaside as children, a British Proustian madeleine.

Their breakfasts are incredible value. Egg and chips is only £2.20, toast will set you back 50p and a tea is only 70p. The fact that the food is so great is really just the icing on the cake, given that the place in which it is served is so lovely and makes it well worth just passing the time here. Smart wooden seats with dark leatherette are arranged around yellow formica-topped wooden tables, faded slightly in the cafe's bright windows, ageing them in a genteel, handsome fashion. We will return here many times.

SEA SHELL
OF LISSON GROVE

Address

49–51 Lisson Grove
Marylebone
NW1 6UH

Telephone

020 7224 9000

Sea Shell has had a recent makeover, both in appearance and quality. In fact, although it has long been a proponent of sustainably caught fish, its dedication to this, in recently aligning themselves with celebrity chef Hugh Fearnley-Whittingstall and Channel 4's *Fish Fight* supporting British fishing communities and techniques that don't deplete fishing stocks, has meant that Sea Shell's fish is reliably fresh and therefore incredibly tasty, as well as ethically sound. Fish to look out for on the menu are Dover Sole, sourced from Cornwall, and salmon and scampi, both from Scotland. The popular chip shop regulars—cod, haddock and plaice—are carefully sourced from monitored stocks in the north-eastern Atlantic so, although such favourites are often to be avoided on ethical grounds, here they are guilt-free.

Sea Shell is divided into a sit-down restaurant and a takeaway, and their outputs are priced accordingly, with a dish in the newly styled restaurant on average £10 higher than their takeaway equivalent. The takeaway has one of the best selections of fish of any takeaway in London. The lemon sole goujons melt in the mouth and the whitebait is crunchy and moreish. A surprise option was the skate wing with chips—a meatier fish than cod or haddock and a good, filling alternative. With Regent's Park, London Zoo, Abbey Road and the Lord's Cricket Ground within walking distance, Sea Shell is well-placed to catch visitors with diverse interests coming through the nearby Marylebone train station, whether they require a full evening meal or a quick snack of whitebait.

FAMILY FISH BOX

SEA SHELL

£12.95

FRESH FISH & CHIPS

PLEURONECTES PLATESSA

SEA SHELL
RESTAURANT

THIS WAY

TOFF'S
OF MUSWELL HILL

Set in leafy and well-heeled Muswell Hill, Toff's—formerly Mr Toff's—is a family run fish & chip restaurant and takeaway that has been in existence for a very respectable 45 years. Despite fish & chips' presence in all corners of London, Toff's is a very much a north London institution. Fish can be cooked in Matzo meal—as well as the usual battering, frying and grilling—and served with vast dill pickles, subtle elements reflecting the large local Jewish population. Matzo turns out to be a good choice: crunchier than batter, it protects the flesh, letting the flaky white haddock steam in its crusty shell, producing a succulently fresh tasting dish.

The current owners Costa and George Georgiou—Greek brothers who took over in 1999—have kept this cherished local treasure true to its original aesthetic. The wood panelled interior is cosy yet grand, set off with large mirrors and vintage photographs of the area, which add to the feeling of being in a restaurant-cum-timewarp. It is the kind of place that in years past families would make an event of visiting and still feel at home.

The takeaway is always busy, but with fish fried quickly in groundnut oil it won't take long to get served. For the real experience, make time to eat in the restaurant. You will join a long list of celebrities, though whoever you are you will be made to feel as though, in Toff's fan Maureen Lipman's words, "they care". They even offer chip top-ups!

Address

38 Muswell Hill Broadway
Muswell Hill
N10 3RT

Telephone

020 8365 2540

TWO BROTHERS

Address

297–303 Regent's Park Road
Finchley
N3 1DP

Telephone

020 8346 0469

Located in a residential area just a short walk down Regent's Park Road from Finchley Central Tube station, Two Brothers is a family business that has run for 24 years, providing a sit-in fishy extravaganza for both its fiercely loyal customers and fortuitous visitors. The space is huge, accommodating around 80 covers. Despite this, the lines on Friday night are the stuff of legend, particularly for the takeaway fish & chips. Everything is fried fresh, evidently something for which the locals consider worth waiting for.

An immensely popular dish is Tony's Arbroath Smokies: hot-smoked haddock in a cream sauce with fresh tomato and cheese. Specials such as mussels with lemon, white wine and parsley and pan-fried cod are also worth mentioning.

Dining here, there is a great feeling of community; staff and customers get absorbed in commenting on the local news, many seem to know each other, giving advice on local know-how such as how to keep your car safe, along with what to order.

Terry's Cafe

SOUTH LONDON

BRADY'S FISH RESTAURANT

Brady's Fish Restaurant is a family run establishment just opposite Wandsworth Town railway station on Old York Road; a haven of hospitality, fresh food and nostalgic favourites.

Luke (with fish opposite) and Amelia Brady have a long history in catering. Luke's grandfather owned and ran the Railway Inn in Brixton from 1909, which was always known as "Brady's" by the locals. It became a chain of pubs and off licences, which Luke and Amelia ran prior to opening a Country House hotel and restaurant in Suffolk. After four years spent missing London, nostalgic for the kinds of food he knew as a child from trips to Pinney's in Suffolk and later, places like Geales in Notting Hill, Luke had something of an epiphany one morning in 1990, saying, "I've got it, we will open a fish & chip shop!" And with that, a new incarnation of Brady's was born.

All that acquired restaurant knowledge has made Brady's a long-standing local gem. The key to the restaurant's success is undoubtedly the fresh fish, which they buy directly from source: cod, haddock, coley and plaice from Grimsby, and other flat fish from Newlyn in Cornwall. Brady's customers get the freshest possible sustainable fish, grilled or fried, at the best possible prices—something of a winning formula, as it has now won *Time Out*'s Best Budget Meal. A final note: save room for dessert after your fish—you will not regret a home-made bread pudding with custard.

Address

513 Old York Road
Wandsworth
SW18 1TF

Telephone

020 8877 9599

FISH CLUB

Address

189 St John's Hill
Clapham Junction
SW11 1TH

Telephone

020 7978 7115

Address

57 Clapham High Street
Clapham
SW4 7TG

Telephone

020 7720 5853

This much loved Clapham fish bar—one of *Time Out London*'s best 50 restaurants of 2011—claims to bring traditional fish & chips into the twenty-first century. In a time when modern fishing should equal sustainability, Fish Club sells seasonally sourced fish delivered fresh twice a day from fishermen based in Mersea Island and Poole. Sheer logic fuels their ecological concern too: their business will last only as long as there are fish in the sea.

The establishment's wet fish counter proudly showcases sustainable alternatives such as coley, and more specialist dishes: the sardines from the Mediterranean and prawn and chorizo kebabs are not to be missed. Down to earth, knowledgeable staff will assist you in the difficult task of choosing what to eat and how to eat it. If the absence of a fish puzzles you, bear in mind that their menu changes with the seasons: native oysters are only available between September and April, while plaice should not be fished between January and March.

This brightly lit, aquarium-themed restaurant is a common takeaway destination for many locals, but you can sit in and enjoy your fish & chips for the same price. Haddock costs £7.70 and coley £6.70; do like everyone else around you and order their sweet potato chips, a side dish hero. Home-made sauces and home-baked bread will complete your fine 'chippy' dining experience—even with table service if you frequent their second shop at Clapham High Street.

GAMBARDELLA

Founded in 1927 and still Sicilian owned and run, Gambardella's is therefore resolutely closed on Sundays. But any other day of the week you will always get a true Italian warm welcome from the owners James and Alex Petrillo. The locals who dine here regularly all seem to know each other and engage in pleasant chat, despite often sitting at separate tables and reading their newspapers while they eat their freshly cooked breakfasts, which are huge and very reasonably priced. A sausage, egg, bacon, chips and beans came to £3.50 and a bacon omelette with chips cost £3.30. This is probably the only place in London where you can still get a cup of tea for 50p.

Alex and James inherited the cafe from their uncle Nicholas, who ran it in the 1960s and who in turn inherited it from his father, Andrew Gambardella, an ice-cream maker from Naples. More than just a cafe, Gambardella's is an institution in Blackheath. It was considered so much a part of true cafe tradition in the UK that it was chosen as the backdrop for a number of Heinz ketchup adverts.

As featured in the advert, the interior is a crucial attraction of Gambardella's. Almost a film set, it is a cross between a Deco 1930s and a more colourful formica 1960s interior, with veneered bucket seats, an orange counter, marble-effect wall panels and an original coffee machine. The staff proudly showed us a copy of *Vogue* featuring a shoot done here. *Playboy* is next month. This cafe has clearly seen a lot in its time.

Address

47–48 Vanbrugh Park
Blackheath
SE3 7JQ

Telephone

020 8858 0327

INSTANT COFFEE	·70 MUG	1·00
TEA	·50 MUG	·80
HERBAL TEA	·60 MUG	·90
HOT CHOCOLATE		1·30
ICED COFFEE FRAPPÉ		2·00
ICED VANILLA FRAPPÉ		2·00
MILKSHAKE		1·50

~CHOCOLATE/STRAWBERRY/BANANA~

MASTERS SUPER FISH

Address

191 Waterloo Road
Waterloo
SE1 8UX

Telephone

020 7928 6924

Considered by some to be one of the few 'real' chippies in the capital, Masters Super Fish is an understated place not too far from Waterloo Station on Waterloo Road. The interior is simple, with coral coloured table tops and spearmint walls decorated with photographs of seafood and black and white images of notable local faces.

Fish is purchased daily from Billingsgate Market. There is an amazing variety sold, from sardines and swordfish to sea bass and skate, and various specials, all of which are served grilled, allowing the taste of the fish to shine. Portions are generous; this is especially true of their cod, which is a local favourite and is of course served traditionally, deep fried in groundnut oil alongside chips and salad. Given the quality of the fare, Masters Super Fish is amazing value. The cod and chips is only £8 and adding half chips / half salad still comes to under £10. There is a brief kids menu and classic sides—mushy peas, green salad and coleslaw.

The takeaway station is also popular, especially in the summer. But beware, like many traditional chippies it closes in the afternoon for an hour and a half between 3 and 4.30 pm. It is also closed on Sundays.

MARIES CAFE

Address

90 Lower Marsh
Waterloo
SE1 7AB

Telephone

020 7928 1050

Maries is perhaps the most unusual cafe to be included in this book as it doubles as a great little Thai restaurant, serving both standard cafe fare (done very well and to a reliably high standard) and a number of curries, Thai dim sum and spicy meat dishes.

As it is open both early and late—from 8 am until 10 pm—it is conceivable to both start and end the day's meals here. Maries doesn't have a liquor license and therefore permits you to bring your own alcohol—corkage is only £1.

From the street, Maries' charming sign invites you in. Cute typography sits alongside an image of a steaming teacup. The interior is reflective of the cafe's dual fare. There are things that are undeniably 'classic cafe' about it—formica table tops, a chalk board full of cafe classics, an old tea boiler—but also things that remind one more of its other offerings. Thai ephemera pops up unexpectedly on the walls and the padded chairs are more local Thai restaurant than cafe. Food is incredibly reasonably priced, however, meaning that whatever you go here for—we had two teas and a portion of beans on toast for £3.40—you will leave with change. This, coupled with the low BYO rates if you are alcohol-inclined, makes the cafe a really good spot for a cheap meal only a brief distance from Waterloo station.

MY TEA SHOP

Address

23 Duke Street Hill
Southwark
SE1 2SW

My Tea Shop is actually Ilir Shala and Zen Sherifi's tea, coffee, breakfast and lunch spot, slotted under a tiny railway arch in London Bridge. Heading out of the station on Duke Street Hill, take a left towards the bridge itself and you will find this tiny, well-loved cafe with an unconventional frontage, which despite its popularity does not seat more than 16 inside.

The interior is bijou and distinctive: a low curved ceiling swoops down at such an angle as to forcibly seat you in the small wood-effect banquette seats either side of the entrance way. Space is tight but the regulars don't mind squeezing in and sharing tables. Ilir told us about fans of the cafe who come back here from Australia every year. Celebrities such as Gordon Ramsay and Graham Norton have also been known to pop in. But famous or not, they like to get to know their customers by name.

There has been a cafe in this location since the 1930s, making it the oldest in the neighbourhood. Ilir and Zen stress the importance of sourcing locally, contributing to trade and providing customers with the freshest ingredients. Their thick and tasty sandwiches are made from sliced crusty bloomer and herb sausages sourced from nearby Borough Market. It is fascinating to see what is possible to produce in such a small space, and well worth a visit after a busy morning checking out Borough Market or walking along the river.

OLLEY'S

Olley's has been voted by the *Evening Standard* as London's best fish & chips—no small praise, given the number of good fish & chips shops in the capital. And indeed it was one of the best we tried. The menu featured a number of variations on the usual fish & chips, such as hake, halibut and sardines, and everything can be done either grilled or fried and with a number of different sides varying in nutritional value, from chips to boiled potatoes and salad.

Set on the Herne Hill end of Norwood Road, this popular wooden villa-style restaurant and takeaway faces onto beautiful Brockwell Park. On a nice day locals often get takeaway and cross the street to sit in the sunshine. Classic cod and chips was one of the chunkiest and flakiest we sampled in all of our research. The batter on the fish was crisp and the chip portions were large without being impossible to finish. We also had calamari to start, which was perfectly soft and well cooked without being at all rubbery. A delicious tartare sauce accompanied it all.

We sat in the window, surrounded by greenery and flowers, which makes the place really welcoming from the street. Inside the space is warm and inviting, with a combination of terracotta tiling, brickwork and exposed wood. With two floors and lots of tables hidden in and around corners it gets loud with full tables of regulars in the evenings. All in all, Olley's is well worth the trip south.

Address

65–69 Norwood Road
Herne Hill
SE24 9AA

Telephone

020 8671 8259
020 8671 5665

MIND THE
STEPS
PLEASE

REGENCY CAFE

This cafe trades off its traditional decor as much as its food; it is a crucial location in a number of films and TV series, most recently the film adaptation of Graham Greene's *Brighton Rock*, where the cafe is featured as the classic 1950s cafe to which Pinkie and Rose disappear together. Its walls are covered in stills from this and other films, such as *Layer Cake*, *Judge John Deed* and *Rescue Me*. The cream tiled walls with black accent tiles are also set off with a number of vintage posters from nearby Tate Britain. Everything about it oozes classic cafe appeal; indeed, from the outside Regency Cafe even looks like Edward Hopper's *Nighthawks*—an aesthetic that has come to epitomise the 'classic cafe'.

There is an unspoken etiquette at Regency Cafe that should be immediately understood on entering. There was a permanent queue when we were there. You must order at the counter and pay before finding a seat. Remember what you ordered and who you ordered after, so that you don't inadvertently collect someone else's order when it is called (or yelled very loudly by Claudia, the owner). Things move quickly here, so if there aren't any booths or seats free, order anyway: like magic, one will likely become available before your food arrives. The kitchen churns out very high quality classic cafe favourites—an array of cooked breakfasts and on Fridays some of the chunkiest fish & chips we have seen.

Address

17–19 Regency Street
Pimlico
SW1P 4BY

Telephone

020 7821 6596

SOMETHING FISHY

Just off the busy market in Lewisham that noisily sells
everything from peaches to polyester leopard-skin rugs
sits a cafe serving proper fish & chips and pie and mash
to its loyal customers. You can't miss Something Fishy:
its bright frontage, though distinctive, belies its interior
space, which is huge and regularly packed. One gets
the impression that it maintains its level of custom all
day, serving everyone from the market stall workers
to the frequenters of the local shops—next door is a
pawnbrokers and a Savers health and beauty store—to
those popping through this part of town on their way
to somewhere else. Everyone is there for the food, the
likes of which it is hard to find in London these days.
It is so authentic they even do jellied eels—a proper
London experience.

Fish & chips are served in a variety of sizes, from a
small cod at £3.50 to a large portion with chips at a very
reasonable £7.25. Haddock, skate, battered sausages
and pies feature heavily. This is likely to be one of the
very few places left in the capital where you can buy the
classic combination of eels, mash and liquor—a bargain
at £4.90. Although modernised somewhat, its clientele
and character feel old-school. It is possible to order at
the counter and eat your dinner at the formica tables,
watching the market jostling outside—an oasis in this
busy and slightly gruff area of town.

Address

117–119 Lewisham
High Street
Lewisham
SE13 6AT

Telephone

020 8852 7075

TERRY'S

Terry's is named after its original owner, Terry Yardley, who was the current owner, Austin's, dad. This cute little cafe is a true old London relic and neatly preserved from an era when cafes were real destinations for those eating out in the capital. Terry was a true Londoner, raised around the bomb sites of post-war South London, and really knew his traditional British food, having started out in his working life in Smithfield meat market at 17 and eventually setting up the cafe in 1982. Now run by Austin, the cafe still produces home cooked food using the best meat from Smithfield market and vegetables and other produce from Borough Market.

Entering the cafe is to walk into a beautiful time warp. Antique union jacks sweep down across large windows, which light up the rows and rows of old photographs documenting the local area and Austin and Terry's family. A sign reads: "when you start to use this cafe you are not just a customer you are a member of a club, a very exclusive club". And this is the feeling the place emanates. Food is served in large portions and locals happily eat it at the gingham coated tables, creating a pleasant hubbub.

The menu features traditional cafe fare, unusual to find in the area today, such as meat pudding and corned beef, alongside the ever popular all day breakfast, known as "The Works". The ploughman's platter is huge, with pie, salad, cheese and hams. The meat pudding a classic suet treat, served traditionally, with two veg and potatoes.

Address

158 Great Suffolk Street
Southwark
SE1 1PE

Telephone

0207 407 9358

THE FLYING FISH

The Flying Fish is a good local fish & chip shop where the staff know what they are serving and are happy to advise on specials. All the fish is fresh and cooked to order. You can even buy your fish—any of many varieties such as plaice, rock, haddock, and other lesser-known species—'wet' (or raw to the rest of us), so that you can cook them at home. Mr Kemal, the owner, is happy to advise on the best fish, fresh from Billingsgate, to barbeque, grill or bake. With some notice he will order in accordingly.

The Flying Fish has a welcome BYO policy. Behind the takeaway section is a small but perfectly formed restaurant with simple tables and chairs, and all the usual condiments and seasonings to hand that you would expect. Prices are decent: a large cod and chips is only £8.50 to eat in and £7 to take away. The chips here are fantastically tasty, and batter is thickly slathered on the fish, leaving the flesh beautifully steamed inside its golden jacket. There is a large area that seats up to 30—a good place for a big family gathering, especially since they offer children's portions of most dishes at knock-down prices. For a really retro experience try their prawn cocktail: at £3.50 it's a great way to kick off a very good meal.

Address

55 Camberwell Church St
Camberwell
SE5 8TR

Telephone

020 7701 7032

THE PHOENIX

Address

441 Goldharbour Lane
Brixton
SW9 8LN

Telephone

020 7733 4430

Despite a couple of recent renovations, The Phoenix is still considered a classic cafe, not least because of its status as the oldest running establishment of its kind in south London, founded in 1928. The previous owner updated the place quite a lot. Behind the kitchen area is now a series of close-up photographs of graffiti, in keeping with Brixton's grittier contemporary scene, which sits alongside the restaurant's more classic fittings. Elsewhere, however, it remains untouched. A regular, Charlie—aged 96—who has been visiting The Phoenix for the last 90 years must recognise much of the interior from his early visits.

The cafe has seen some sights over the years. The little back room was used as an illicit gambling den in the 1930s and still houses two small tables. The giant tea boiler has been here since then as well, as have the large mirrors on the walls which make this small place seem bigger.

Thanks to nearby, newly trendy Brixton Market, the area has changed a great deal and the current owner is under pressure to modernise much of the interior. Aware of its classic status, he is sensitive of the desire to keep much of its cherished history present in the re-fit.

THE SEA COW

Address

37 Lordship Lane
East Dulwich
SE22 8EW

Telephone

020 8693 3111

The Sea Cow is a favourite with local Dulwich families due to the fact that children eat for free before 4 pm at weekends. As a result it is usually extremely busy over Saturday and Sunday lunchtimes. For those wanting a more peaceful eating experience it is a good idea to come to this clean, comfortable and gentrified chippy in the evenings, when The Sea Cow has its deal with Green and Blue, the great wine emporium across the road, allowing you to take your food to their bar in a kind of inverse BYO policy. This way you can get fantastic fish & chips with an excellent bottle of wine way above usual restaurant standards for a very reasonable price.

Like many successfully reinvigorated fish & chip shops, The Sea Cow does more than just the generic fare. It ticks all the boxes for sustainable and ethical policies, provides a nice atmosphere and very high standards of food, including such menu items as whole gilt head bream, grilled sardines and tiger prawns. The staff are knowledgeable and will tell you about both the fish varieties and their provenance, which is handy given that some are unusual and atypical of your standard chip shop. The interior aims to be a combination of "old English beach hut and Sydney chic" with an open airy feel and large, shared tables made from bare, heavy oak with benches along each side. Aesthetic elements such as the life rings on the walls can seem a little reductive to the otherwise sharp, utilitarian design, but mostly The Sea Cow gets it spot on.

the sea cow

0208 693 3111

the sea cow

KIDS
eat free!
Weekends til 4pm
Come and see inside for details

FIRS

WOODEN CHIP FORKS

Strike a li...
...... ITS C...

YOU'VE NEVER H...
SO CHIPPED !

PUDS

make
some room!

For those with room to spare, something to follow.

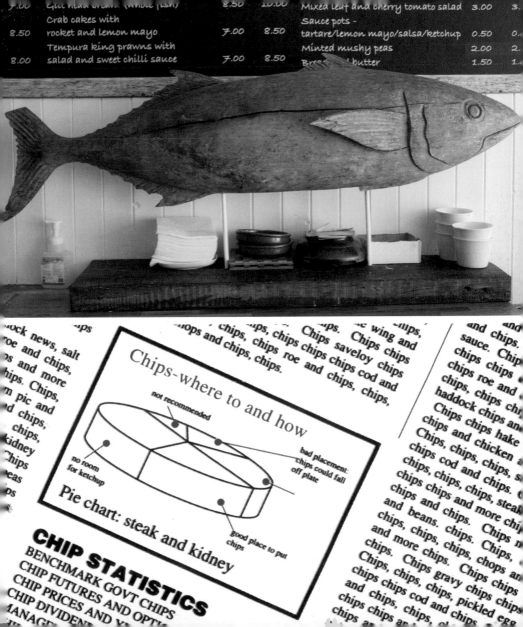

		Crab cakes with			Mixed leaf and cherry tomato salad	3.00	3.
8.50		rocket and lemon mayo	7.00	8.50	Sauce pots - tartare/lemon mayo/salsa/ketchup	0.50	0.
		Tempura king prawns with			Minted mushy peas	2.00	2.
8.00		salad and sweet chilli sauce	7.00	8.50	Bread and butter	1.50	1.

...ps ...ock news, salt ...roe and chips, ...s and chips, ...hips and more ...Chips, ...m pie and ...d chips, ...chips, ...kidney ...Chips ...eas ...ps

...chips, ...hops ...chips, chips, ...hops and chips, chips. ...chips chips roe and chips, chips,

Chips. Chips saveloy chips cod and chips, chips,

wing and ...ps. ...e wing and

and ...and chips. ...sauce. Chip ...chips chips ...chips roe and ...chips, chips chips ...haddock chips an ...Chips chips hake ...chips and chicken a ...Chips, chips, chips, ...chips cod and chips, s ...chips, chips, chips, ...chips chips, chips, steak ...chips and more chip ...and beans. chips. Chips ...chips, chips, chips, ...and more chips. Chips, ...chips. Chips gravy chips chips ...Chips, chips, chips, ...chips chips cod and chips ...and chips, chips, ...chips chips, chips, of ...chips a...

Chips-where to and how

not recommended

no room for ketchup

bad placement: chips could fall off plate

good place to put chips

Pie chart: steak and kidney

CHIP STATISTICS
BENCHMARK GOVT CHIPS
CHIP FUTURES AND OPTI...
CHIP PRICES AND ...
CHIP DIVIDEN...
MANAGE...

TONY'S CAFÉ

Address

11 Chapter Street
Westminster
SW1P 4NY

Telephone

020 7630 5270

The exterior of Tony's Café has recently had a face-lift, repainted in black with the addition of "Tony's Café" in gold lettering, allowing it to fit in nicely with the smart street on which it sits. The interior, however, has remained unchanged for the 67 years it has been open. Among the most beautiful features are the bright orange decorated tiles that sit behind the kitchen area. The tables have lovely mottled blue tops and all the seating is in booths for four, in faded red leatherette. In truth, Tony's is one of the most aesthetically 'classic' of all the cafes featured in this book. Although worn, the cafe is one of the most charming we have visited.

The menu board features an array of fare, from pies and the expected breakfasts to liver, mixed grills and tempting home-made casseroles. For pudding they offer a variety of pancakes, with toppings and flavour combinations hailing from different parts of the world.

TONY'S

You can't miss the bright yellow frontage of this well-known local institution, the last worker's cafe left on the smart and trendy Northcote Road. The interior has brown leatherette padded seating and formica table tops slotted into every available space, sometimes making squeezing around the cafe tricky, especially given the sprawling lunch time crowd, comprising a cross-section of the local population, from students to pensioners.

Tony's does a range of all-day breakfasts, as well as a series of specials, such as lamb dinner with three veg, and liver, bacon, mash and onions, both of which come with huge quantities of gravy. There are novelty salt and pepper shakers in abundance along with the other familiar condiments of ketchup, brown sauce and mustard. Tony's looks after its regular clientele, many of whom come for the old-fashioned meals of pies and roasts and sit quietly in the booths with their newspapers, seemingly oblivious to the world. Tony Kose welcomes everyone with friendly conversation and a beaming smile. As I reach for my tea I get the presumably oft-used spiel, "Sugar's here, but I think you're sweet enough darling."

Apparently, though unsurprisingly for the area, Tony's remit now diversifies in the evening. Full Turkish mezes are available, and the cafe has a BYO policy; the low prices mean that this is probably the best value meal in an increasingly expensive part of south London.

Address

74 Northcote Road
Wandsworth
SW11 6QW

Telephone

020 7228 0929

Poppies

EAST LONDON

ARTHUR'S CAFÉ

Address

495 Kingsland Road
Dalston
E8 4AU

Telephone

020 7254 3391

Arthur's Café sits on that stretch of Kingsland Road which, although right across from the huge new development around Dalston Junction station, manages to retain some of its traditional shops such as the haberdashers William Gee and Sons. Arthur's' tiled frontage with cursive orange sign feels at home here, adding retro charm to this area at war with its own gentrification. Serving as proof that people love the area's tradition and character, Arthur's is always packed and the general chatter of this bustling place only adds to the already buzzing atmosphere of busy Kingsland Road.

Arthur's is named after 85-year-old Arthur (pictured left), who is part of London's die-hard cafe community —friends with the Pellicis, he worked in a number of similar establishments prior to opening his own when he was 21. In short Arthur's seems to have been around forever, rather than just since 1932. It's a bubbly family affair, and now co-owned with his grandson James (pictured right), the cafe does a great trade in both delicious sandwiches and cakes to take away and full sit-down meals. Arthur is an important presence in the cafe, impeccably dressed in his white coat, shaking hands with all his regulars and serving his huge portions of home-made meat, veg and gravy with charm and grace. He gets up as early as 1 am to cook the food from scratch. Breakfast stops at 11.30 am on the dot and to mark the change between breakfast and lunch, Arthur changes into a clean coat. For fans of a builder's brew it is worth noting that Arthur's does a very strong cup of tea—a great pick-up on a rainy London day.

Arthur's Cafe

PHONE ORDERS TAKEN
020 7254 3391

EST. 1935

495 KINGSLAND RD
HACKNEY LONDON E8 4AU

FRESHLY CUT SANDWICHES MADE TO ORDER

FILLINGS	SANDWICHES BAP F/STICK	WITH SALAD	ROLLS	WITH SALAD	BEVERAGES	
BACON/SAUSAGE	£2.25	£2.60	£1.50	£1.90	TEA	90p
BEEF	£2.10	£2.60	£1.40	£1.75	ALL MILK COFFEE	£1.10
BOILED EGG	£1.70	£2.20	£1.30	£1.65	HOT CHOC	£1.10
CHEESE	£2.00	£2.50	£1.35	£1.70	LEMON TEA	£1.00
CORNED BEEF	£2.10	£2.60	£1.40	£1.75	MILK / HOT MILK	90p
FRIED EGG	£1.70	£2.20	£1.30	£1.65	BOVRIL	85p
HAM	£2.10	£2.60	£1.40	£1.75	COKE	70p
HAM & CHEESE	£2.45	£2.95	£1.60	£1.95	DIET COKE	70p
LIVER SAUSAGE	£2.10	£2.60	£1.40	£1.75	RIBENA	70p
PRAWN	£2.40	£2.90	£1.50	£1.85	7 UP	70p
PORK	£2.10	£2.60	£1.40	£1.75	RIO	70p
SALMON	£2.40	£2.90	£1.50	£1.85	PERRIER	70p
SMOKED SALMON	£2.60	£3.10	£1.60	£1.95	BOTTLED WATER	80p
SALAMI	£2.10	£2.60	£1.40	£1.75	OASIS	£1.20
TUNA	£2.30	£2.80	£1.45	£1.80	LUCOZADE	£1.00
TURKEY	£2.10	£2.60	£1.40	£1.75	FRESH ORANGE GLASS	£1.00
BACON & EGG	£2.75	£3.25	£1.95	£2.30	FRESH ORANGE BOTTLE	90p
BACON & SAUSAGE	£2.75	£3.25	£1.95	£2.30	APPLE JUICE BOTTLE	90p
SAUSAGE & EGG	£2.75	£3.25	£1.95	£2.30	SAN PELLEGRINO	£1.00
EXTRAS	30p	30p	25p	25p		

BEPPE'S CAFÉ

Beppe's is perfectly placed next to Smithfield Market, London's last surviving wholesale meat market, housed in a beautiful Grade II listed building. Not for vegetarians, the market is nonetheless well worth a visit during its bustling morning activity. The area is now also home to many city offices and a number of London's famous nightclubs, such as Fabric, making it a great place to see a huge cross-section of London's population within a short time span, and all in Beppe's Sandwich Bar. Early on the clubbers arrive for some sustenance before bed, followed by market workers after a hard shift, then city bankers for breakfast and coffee and just about everyone for lunch.

Outside Beppe's there's a very retro box 'snack bar' sign, complete with steaming cuppa, signalling the 'classic' cafe to be found within. Aficionados will not be disappointed—red leatherette seating and cork effect wall panels, along with the family portraits, will delight any classic cafe fan. Although they are known for their slightly gruff service, the place is always packed. For a warm welcome, however, go for a cup of tea or a classic Italian meal after the busy lunchtime. Everyone's favourite dish here is said to be steak and kidney pie, but the sandwiches, pastas and daily specials are also worth trying.

Address

23 West Smithfield
EC1A 9HY

Telephone

020 7733 4430

CAFE BLISS

Address

9 Dalston Lane
Dalston
E8 3DF

Telephone

020 7254 4954

Cafe Bliss has possibly the best classic cafe sign we have seen to go with its excellent name: "hot meals our speciality " on a bright yellow background with a happy chef's face. Indeed, the feeling continues inside, creating an atmosphere that pulls in locals and workers all morning and lunchtime. The place is inviting. The floor is that kind of dark, deep red colour that sets off the dark wood panelling and other decor beautifully. The booths are made from wood and black leatherette, contrasting with the greenish granite-effect formica table tops; the place manages to be bright, welcoming and warm all at the same time. A new paint job inside makes it clean and fresh without feeling too new. Cafe Bliss has a resolutely retro-classic design interior largely unseen these days. And although the new lime green exterior frontage is a bit bright, at least it makes its presence known amid Dalston Lane's hipster-filled coffee joints. Its name is justified as an antidote to the busy street—Bliss.

Our baked potato was a faultless example of an admittedly common dish: generous, well-seasoned, crispy and soft in all the right places and coated in a mound of melting cheese. Nearby, men in high visibility jackets packed the booths and devoured huge and tasty looking mixed grills, the frying of which forms the background noise to the usual cafe chatter. The cafe also serves fish at a very reasonable price: excellent dishes of cod with chips and peas, and scampi are only £4 and £4.30, respectively.

CITY CORNER

Address

210 Middlesex Street
Whitechapel
E1 7JF

Telephone

020 7283 6247

Delfina Cordani set up the City Corner cafe in June 1963 with her husband Giuseppe, who she met at the Italian church in Clerkenwell. The seating inside still consists of darkish greeny-blue banquettes and everything is covered in a wood pattern effect. The seats are decidedly 1960s, small and at a narrow fixed-distance to the tables, so eating too much here too often could potentially prevent a return, eventually.

Given its location in the city, virtually opposite Liverpool Street station, and with a steady trickle of city workers through its doors, it is not hard to imagine the deals brokered across its tables over the years, the novels written and the arguments had and settled. Its warmth and character is a million miles from that of many generic London cafes and the food is freshly cooked with a menu full of traditional British dishes and a few Italian favourites.

The Cordanis have their original WM Still and Son coffee machine on the cramped bar. It still works perfectly, both at making coffee and instantly transporting the customer back into the aura of 1960s London.

E. PELLICCI

Infamous haunt of deceased gangsters—rumour has it the Kray brothers were fans!—and the antithesis to faceless corporate cafe-culture, E. Pellicci is a prime example of a proper classic 'greasy spoon'. There is no better example of a *bona fide* London institution.

Situated on the ever-bustling Bethnal Green Road, its interior is a haven of charmingly antiquated marquetry and an English Heritage Grade II listed Art Deco treat created in 1946 by local carpenter Achille Capocci. From the street the cafe stands out with its gloriously evocative and eye-catching primrose Vitrolite facade. Now run by the third generation of Italian emigrant Pellicci's—the most recognisable of whom, Nevio Sr, was born in 1926 to Elide Pellicci in the building's upstairs rooms, and who passed away in 2008—the cafe attracts an extensive range of minor celebrities, East End locals and roaming gastro-cultural enthusiasts. The Pellicci family offer unprecedented warm welcomes to all, which has garnered them staunch dedication from locals.

The menu comprises traditional cafe and Italian staples done consistently well—breakfasts here are particularly gargantuan and lauded by all who consume them. For anyone with some room after a lunch of the Pellicci's famous and delicious lasagne, a slab of bread pudding will complete the meal nicely.

Address

332 Bethnal Green Road
Bethnal Green
E2 0AG

Telephone

020 7739 4873

FAULKNERS

Address

424–426 Kingsland Road
Dalston
E8 4AA

Telephone

020 7254 6152

Faulkners Fish Restaurant is a relic of a distant era in this trendy part of town. While nearby bars and pubs are increasingly serving gastropub food to hipsters, one gets the feeling that Faulkners has no intention of altering its fare or decor. Net curtains, carpet, table cloths and wooden chalet-like walls all add to the feeling that Faulkners was bang on trend in 1970 and has not changed since. And this is its charm, attracting a varied clientele, from elderly couples who eat a regular fish supper every Friday evening to office workers nipping in for a quick lunch and nearby tech and design industry youngsters, who stand around the takeaway *en masse*, chattering excitedly about the latest app and munching Faulkners large, freshly fried chips.

There is both a restaurant with a large capacity and a takeaway stand next door. For diners who choose to eat in the restaurant, prices are not cheap but neither too unreasonable. Skate will set you back £12.90 and salmon £10.90, making them a better deal than the pubs down the road. For those that can't leave their desks for the lunchtime opening hours (noon to 2.30 pm) they even deliver, and the food turns up still crispy and hot. Doing so, however, would mean missing a vital experience of eating filleted and deep fried fish under the watchful gaze of your dinner's distant relations in the prominent tropical fish tank while listening to classic soft rock ballads. On emerging into the Dalston air we had to check our iPhones to make sure this was in fact 2012 and not 1970.

FISH HOUSE

Owners Gabriel Early and Johanna Nylander received their culinary training at the University of the Basque Country, which is one of the reasons Fish House outdoes all of the other fish & chips places in the surrounding area. Their training allows them to operate as both a good local modern fish restaurant and a reliably good fish & chips takeaway.

Victoria Park Village, where the restaurant is situated, has fast become a gentrified and trendy area, becoming progressively more well-heeled as the Olympics have pushed East London into the spotlight. The leafy park itself offers a beautiful location to eat a takeaway; for those who want to dine in, the restaurant, which takes up half of the venue, is contemporary, with glass topped tables and slightly severe looking chairs, which turn out to be really quite comfortable. The restaurant is full of things you might not expect to find in somewhere so known for their good fish & chips. Saffron and lemon seafood risotto, Colchester oysters and a raved-about fish pie are all complemented by tempting English puddings. Traditional fish & chips fans will not be disappointed. Large, chunky cuts of fish are doused in batter and fried fresh, and chips, made from potatoes supplied by local farmers and growers, are hand-cut. To go with a classic haddock and chips, try a "top wally"—a large sweet and sour gherkin.

Address

126–128 Lauriston Road
Victoria Park
E9 7LH

Telephone

020 8533 3327

L. RODI

Address

16 Blackhorse Lane
Walthamstow
E17 6HJ

Telephone

020 8527 4541

It is hard to express the classic heritage of this cafe without referring to Adrian Maddox's "Classic Cafes" website, subsequently printed in Black Dog Publishing's book of the same name. He enthusiastically writes of this place: "the front room is a fantasy of marble-mint formica set under sparkling Vitrolite; chrome-edged tables are packed tight against an original counter with a giant old English Electric fridge at the back.... The back room is a veritable caff museum: lined with emerald and off-white tiles... the place has barely changed in a century. Overwhelming. Emotional. Essential." Indeed, even in 2012, this is the case.

Large mirrors reflect formica as far as the eye can see. And the meals are traditional here, too; chicken escalope and veg, roast lamb and two veg, gammon steak and pineapple all come out of the kitchen to be placed on the orange formica table tops and devoured by local workers.

This cafe has been here since 1925, making it one of the oldest in the book. The tea boiler has probably been churning out hot cuppas since then. Although a little tatty in places, this cafe has been incredibly preserved. Little net curtains still hang in the window, framing the view out to the cars whooshing by on Blackhorse Lane. The drivers would be well advised to pay attention to this ageing cafe, because stunningly preserved decor aside, you can't do much better than a bacon roll for only £1.45.

Luis' Café

LUIS' CAFÉ

Clerkenwell, a historic area in the Borough of Islington, home to famous green spaces such as Lincoln's Inn Fields, has been a popular residential location since the seventeenth century as told by its beautiful terraced architecture and narrow cobbled streets. In the Industrial Revolution it became known for watch-making, but nowadays it is the home of many of London's designers, notably jewellery and furniture design agencies and makers, meaning the local markets on Leather Lane and Exmouth Market are now filled with trendy street-food stands during busy lunch breaks.

Given the overall gentrification to the area, it is a marvel that Luis' still exists. It is a tiny space on Rosebery Avenue near Farringdon Road, measuring no wider than two metres across and drawn into a wedge at its end. As such it only has room for two tables and the packed bar area, stuffed full of sandwiches, cakes and snacks. But despite its diminutive size, the staff manage to produce lunches for the vast numbers of local office workers who crowd in between 12 and 2 pm. Grilled sandwiches are its speciality, filled with roasted vegetables, chicken and various cheeses and herbs.

For a less busy time, though only a little, go and have a cup of tea and a breakfast in the morning. There are a few stools around the bar, fixed to the beige panelled walls, on which to perch. With the influx of the design crowd, it is a relief to find a reasonably priced cup of tea in the area.

Address

25 Rosebery Avenue
Clerkenwell
EC1R 4SP

Telephone

020 7837 1802

POPPIES

Address

6–8 Hanbury Street
Spitalfields
E1 6QR

Telephone

020 7247 0892

Website

poppiesfishandchips.co.uk

Pop and his family have been serving fish & chips in London since 1945. There is a retro feel to this place—fish is presented in 'poppies' newsprint' as was the tradition of East End chippies using up yesterday's newspapers. The serving staff wear authentic fish & chip shop uniforms, adding to the charm of this revamped classic.

Fish is constantly being freshly fried and orders come out quickly, maintaining optimum crispiness. The fish is good, from sustainable sources and in generous portions. The chips are crispy but nothing to write home about compared to the fresh and tasty fish. The restaurant also has an alcohol license, so you can have a beer or a bottle of wine with your meal, from a list including appropriate bottles—the house white is an acceptable Muscadet—and excellent London beers from the Meantime brewery.

It is the convenience of this place that makes it stand out, however. The restaurant is right in the middle of busy Spitalfields and yet it does not cost the earth; you can be in and out in quick time and the food is tasty, hot and served with a smile. Poppies is a fish restaurant that works well.

London's Fires Out But One

By seven o'clock last night London Fire Brigade announced that fires caused by air raids have been overcome or extinguished, with the exception of one which is in hand.

Many bombs were dropped the docks of the Port of London Authority, and a large fire caused in the docks south of river. Elsewhere some warehouses were damaged and several bars were set on fire.

The attacks in other parts London were not comparable magnitude, but many bombs were dropped. In South London schools were seriously damaged fire was caused in Central L

POPPIES
OF SPITALFIELDS

Is it true that the best fish and chips can only be found in the East End? If you ask Pop and his team they can point you to the restaurant and takeaway, full of market workers, the delivery boys and other city folk,

work under bombardment.
In Great Britain, outside London area, the only report major damage comes from an installation on the Lo Thames, where a large fire caused.

These attacks much exceed in scale any that have preced

the showers warmth of their w thunderous applause coach.

BELLS PEA

SCOTTI'S SNACK BAR

Address

39 Clerkenwell Green
Clerkenwell
EC1R 0DU

Telephone

020 7253 8676

Scotti's Snack Bar is a rare find in London. Walking into beautiful Clerkenwell Green, rather interestingly home to both the Karl Marx Memorial Library and the London Masonic Centre, Scotti's is a small, pale cream fronted traditional cafe nestled into the south-west corner. Outside, men sit at tables chatting with staff under the blue awning. Inside, the interior transports the customer into the 1950s. An ornate shelving unit with inbuilt mirrors reflects the customer from behind the perfectly preserved counter. A little glass cabinet with "hot snacks" illuminated on an orange sign sits atop the counter next to an array of thick sliced sandwiches. To the right of the bar is a small gas stove used for making espresso 'the Italian way'. Next to it, a bowl of fresh eggs waits to be cooked. A still life wouldn't represent a more classic image of a 1950s family-run cafe.

Scotti's is not a place for fry-ups but rather does fantastic sandwiches and a great cup of tea or coffee. The menu is not long and sprawling but gets to the point of what this place is about—doing fresh food well. It has been doing much the same thing for 45 years, run by the same family since the current owner's father (pictured left) started it. Traces of their history are proudly displayed along the walls, from little drawings of the cafe to portraits of their relatives and images of their sporting heroes. Sitting at the old wooden furniture against the checkered panelling on the walls and eating a home-made chicken escalope sandwich here is a pleasure.

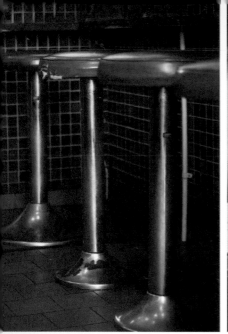

CIABATTA MELTS

HAM + CHEESE —————— 4·70
CHICKEN + CHEESE —————— 4·70
TUNA + CHEESE —————— 4·70
BACON + CHEESE —————— 4·70
CHEESE + MUSHROOM — 4·4C
CHEESE + HAM + MUSHROOM - 5·3
ESCALOPE + CHEESE — 5·5C
STEAK + CHEESE —————— 5·70
MOZZARELLA + TOMATO + OLIVE
AND BASIL —————— 3·80
SALAMI + CHEESE —————— 4·70

LETTUCE / TOMATO / CUCUMBER
MAYO / PICKLE —— 20p E/A
SWISS CHEESE 20p EXTRA

THE REGIS SNACK BAR

Walking into Leadenhall Market is like stepping back in time. It is a gaudily replicated Victorian arcade in steel, filled underneath with shops, pubs and wine bars. Although peppered with smart-suited bankers and the occasional tourist, it is a world away from contemporary office blocks that surround it. You can spot Regis immediately upon entering Leadenhall. After a long wrangling with the city, who wanted them to conform to the surrounding colour scheme, English Heritage came to the rescue, requesting the cafe keep the original wooden frontage. The sign is written in simple, carved wood lettering above the small cafe—a testament to individuality, tradition and a design classic that refuses to conform to a prescribed gentrification format.

The recession has meant that things have changed quickly here. In the past the cafe stayed open later to cater to the Lloyds workers who came to take tea in the afternoon. The pubs pick up the afternoon custom these days, meaning Regis can close at 3 pm—well deserved after their very early morning starts. The owners, brothers Sergio and Dinos, know everyone by their nick-names. No surprise given the longevity of the place. Their parents, Giuseppe and Angela Rapacioli bought it in 1968 from a family member who had been there since the 1950s. There has been a cafe in its location since the 1920s. Although the original tea boiler has been replaced by a smart coffee machine, much of the interior remains charmingly authentic and happily filled with the business chatter of its clientele.

Address

34 Leadenhall Market
EC3V 1LR

Telephone

020 7626 2754

THE SHEPHERDESS

Address

221 City Road
Shoreditch
EC1V 1JN

Telephone

020 7253 2463

The Shepherdess is the kind of cafe you are sure you have been to before. Large windows allow customers to sit for long periods watching the world go by on busy City Road. Unchanged in over 20 years, the cafe has become a familiar backdrop to the goings on in the area, one behind which it is possible to disappear for a while with a cup of tea.

Its location on the corner of Shepherdess Walk gives the cafe its name. The interior is unusually open and airy for a 'classic cafe'. The counters, walls, tables and chairs all look like they belong to different eras, casually thrown together and painted in bright blues and greens as if to cohere them. A hand-written menu board and counters covered in bright signs complete the feel of a well-loved cafe. Diversifying its use somewhat, the cafe now hires itself out as a photoshoot location. On evenings the large windows are sometimes floodlit, while angular models strut and pout behind the counter and photographers snap away. A scene from *Notes on a Scandal* was even filmed here.

The cafe, when it is a working cafe, caters to people from all walks of life, many of whom eat their breakfasts here everyday, though we're not sure if this is to be recommended. Nevertheless for everyone from hungry construction workers to baffled tourists, hurried policemen and frazzled office workers, The Shepherdess is a quiet haven in the local hubbub.

Blandford's

WEST LONDON

BLANDFORD'S

Address

65 Chiltern Street
Marylebone
W1U 6NH

Telephone

020 7486 4117

Rumour has it that this classic Marylebone cafe was a favourite of The Kinks' frontman Ray Davies. Whether this is true or not, legend is certainly what makes Blandford's. This cafe has been providing locals with some of the best breakfasts and bacon sandwiches in the area for 50 years. Recently taken over by Jessica, a Londoner of Italian and Spanish descent, the establishment is undergoing a profound kitchen makeover yet retaining the warm glow of its original furniture and decor.

Cute wooden tables and leatherette seats mix their aged and scuffed character with the impressive wallpaper depicting an old Stockholm harbour scene. This is a place of odd combinations that work pretty well: the menu has maintained its British staples, with a twist courtesy of Jessica's southern European heritage. The HP sauce sits with pastas, stracciatella soup and gazpacho. Flat white fans such as *Monocle* magazine editor-in-chief Tyler Brûlé now go there for their afternoon Italian coffee. This might mean the end of the grease on Blandford's spoon, but Jessica is resolved to keep the family-like spirit alive for the tide of new customers. "Marylebone feels like a village", she says about the borough where she was born and raised. She wants to make sure that people know Blandford's has changed hands, while welcoming all the old regulars to claim their favourite seats, just as they always have.

FRANK'S SANDWICH BAR

Address

Addison Bridge Place
Hammersmith
W14 8XP

Telephone

020 7603 4121

Frank's Sandwich Bar has been family-run for over 50 years. Housed in a converted railway signal box, this narrow establishment is a treasure waiting for those who manage to walk to the upper end of Hammersmith Road without being lured into one of the many restaurants on the way. The cafe utilises its outside pavement in the warmer months (and sometimes the colder ones) to entice you with a few tables and chairs, often occupied by groups of workers on their lunch break. If you pay a visit as early as 6 am on a weekday you will probably find the same scene.

Old-school service and bustling activity are the norm here. Your order—a sandwich, a hot baguette, a salad or a cup of tea, say—will be realised by the men in black T-shirts behind the bar in a clock-work way. The cold sandwiches are made to order in front of you and all food is prepared to take away or served on classic cafe china to eat in. Spare a few minutes and enjoy your fresh food at the diner-style table at the back, or join the solitary customers sitting at the bar that runs the length of the wide window. The wooden surfaces and old mirrors will contribute to your meal's Hopperesque charm.

FRANKS SANDWICH BAR
020 7603 4121

MENU

SANDWICHES
CHEESE £1·70   CORNED BEEF £1·70
EGG MAYO £1·70   LIVER SAUSAGE £1·70
HAM £2·10   BEEF £2·20   CHICKEN £2·20
SPICY TUNA £2·10   TUNA-SWEETCORN £2·10
SMOKED SALMON £2·35   SARDINES £2·20
CREAM CHEESE £2·20   BRIE £2·20
SALAMI £2·10   EGG-TOMATO £1·80
CHEESE-HAM £2·70   B.L.T £2·70
CHICKEN-BACON £2·70   ITALIAN CHICKEN £2·70
CORONATION CHICKEN £2·70

SALADS
MADE TO ORDER FROM £3·50
EAT-IN OR TAKE-AWAY

DRINKS
TEA 80p   COFFEE £1·10
HOT CHOCOLATE £1·20

COLD DRINKS
from 80p

THERE IS A
£1·50
MINIMUM CHARGE
TO EAT IN

HOT SNACKS
2 BACON, EGG, SAUSAGE + BEANS £3·85
EGG, SAUSAGE + BEANS ON 2 TOAST £3·00
EGG + BEANS ON 2 TOAST   £2·65
HOT SANDWICHES AND ROLLS
EGG + BACON £2·15   BACON £2·20
EGG + SAUSAGE £2·10   SAUSAGE £1·70
HOT BAGUETTES
DOUBLE SAUSAGE £2·70   DOUBLE EGG £2·50
BACON £2·80   EGG £3·00
2 SAUSAGE + EGG £3·30   BACON-SAUSAGE £3·20

GINO'S CAPPUCCINO BAR

Address

69 Welbeck Street
Marylebone
W1G 0AT

Telephone

020 7486 7490

The heroic moustache belonging to Gino—the eponymous owner of Gino's Cappuccino Bar—isn't the only thing that's aesthetically pleasing about his stalwart little cafe. Traditional garish signage, faux marble tiling and charming, retro swivel-stools all afford an archetypal 'classic cafe' atmosphere.

The somewhat rudimentary mural of a Full English breakfast above the counter might appear a little incongruous, but the Joan Miró paintings—replicas —and collages of Gino's own customer photos on the walls nicely offset it. The cafe's food is a mix of the *de-rigueur* 'greasy spoon' menu—fry-ups, jacket potatoes, a few cakes—and more continental Italian sandwich bar fare with a large array of cold meats and cheese. Service is reliably quick, a necessary facet given Gino's location next to the bustling commuter thoroughfare of Marylebone Station, so it is no trouble to grab a coffee or meal on the run.

In addition, what discerning, stoic aficionado of old-school London culture would prefer to eat in one of the faceless chains peppering the station concourse rather than this genial, welcoming little independent establishment? Exactly.

GEALES FISH RESTAURANT

Address

2 Farmer Street
Notting Hill
W8 7SN

Telephone

020 7727 7528

Address

1 Cale Street
Chelsea
SW3 3QT

Telephone

0207 965 0555

Famous Geales Fish Restaurant has been a beacon of quality in London's traditional fish & chips scene for more than 70 years. Acquired in 2006 by Concept Venues club and hotel group creators Mark Fuller and Andy Taylor, the restaurant has been refurbished according to the pair's stylish take on fine dining and hospitality. It maintains a rustic feel but with glamorous touches and original features, combined with a young and laid-back service, and a dedication to high quality food. In these times of increasing concern about the exhaustion of maritime resources, Geales use only sustainably caught, seasonally-viable fish. With these, chef Oli Burgess creates classic plates amongst which the beer battered fish & chips are *de rigueur*: pollock will cost you £10.75 and sole £12.50.

Burgess creates echoes of nostalgic seaside trips in his traditional prawn cocktail, crispy deep-fried whitebait and dressed Cornish crab. Geales has joined those who champion scampi as a sustainable alternative to other seafood; their deep fried version waves its 'pub food' flag without shame. There are prime cuts of beef for those unreceptive to fish, and an array of desserts that will delight those brave souls with some room after the sumptuous oceanic parade. A recently opened second restaurant in Chelsea is testament to Geales' success. Rumour has it that a third is on its way.

GEORGE'S PORTOBELLO FISH BAR

Greek-Cypriot George Periccos opened his fish bar on Portobello Road in 1961. Cherished by locals, tourists and foodies from all over the world, it is also apparently Jamie Oliver's favourite chippy; as indicated by the *Observer Food Monthly* feature framed on the wall. Myriad other reviews and magazine cuttings dotted around indicate the achievements of this Portobello landmark. George's Fish Bar is, after all, an institution—the Chelsea FC youth team is often to be seen there queuing for their after-training dinner.

Located in a comparatively quiet spot, the American-style bar, with its neon signs, shiny metal surfaces and coloured tiles is as striking as it is inexpensive. Cod, skate and haddock are sourced from Billingsgate Fish Market. A portion of fish & chips with sweet mushy peas will cost you the attractive sum of £4.50. The price hints at the fact that there is no sit-in restaurant: your fish will be prepared for you to take away. However, they do have some tables outside which are extremely popular on sunny days. If for any reason you do not feel like sampling the fish, then spare ribs, burgers, kebabs, baked potatoes and smoothies are also available: a hearty fast-food emporium that will please all.

Address

329 Portobello Road
Notting Hill
W10 5SA

Telephone

020 8969 7895

HICKEY'S CAFE REST

Goldhawk locals can pride themselves on having an official Hammersmith landmark as their all-day dining neighbourhood cafe. Established in 1948, the place has had a face-lift since it was recently taken over from Louis and Elle Prodromou, who had owned it for 57 years. The current owners, Patrick Hickey (pictured right) and Karen McLoughlin, have brought more light—as well as a new coffee machine—into the place, and are working hard to keep it open most of their waking day, seven days a week.

Patrick will tell you how Cafe Rest was in the top five of London cafes in the 1990s and, with the BBC headquarters located at walking distance, how the place regularly hosted the meals of British TV stars such as Richard and Judy. This is the kind of cafe where regulars are generations of locals; indeed, workers and pensioners having lunch look pretty much at home here.

The new frontage has been newly painted bright green and bears the sign "free WiFi", bringing Cafe Rest bang up to date. Though inside, it retains much of its original classic charm, such as the old wooden furniture and the identical Heinz condiment sets. The menu features straightforward comfort food, with all the British staples and an Irish touch brought by Patrick and Karen straight from Co. Tipperary. Go on a Sunday for the real feast, when families gather to enjoy their Irish roast—a rare opportunity to see London's good old times alive and bustling.

Address

39 Goldhawk Road,
Shepherds Bush
W12 8QQ

Telephone

0871 971 7860

KERBISHER & MALT

Address

53 New Broadway
Ealing
W5 5AH

Telephone

020 8840 4418

Address

164 Shepherds Bush Road
Shepherds Bush
W6 7PB

Telephone

020 3556 0228

Website

www.kerbisher.co.uk

"No to preservatives, no to food from a packet, no to dirty oil, no to neon lights and no to soggy chips." With these laudable principles, ex-Oxo Tower chef Saul Reuben and his brother-in-law Nick Crossley set up the project that is luring excited fish fans into these two quiet spots in Brook Green and Ealing. Kerbisher & Malt are sleek, immaculate shops practising the simple aim to provide the freshest ethically-sourced fish, cooking it to order and serving it with hand-cut humble looking chips, all bathed in home-made sauces and dips.

Shiny white tiles, a stout, communal wooden table in the centre, and environmentally friendly packaging reveal Kerbisher & Malt's aspiration to be the traditional chip shop that never existed—namely, one so ethically minded that it turns their vegetable oil into biofuel. Their traditional-gone-vintage ethos has conquered locals, businessmen, mothers and food critics alike. It is no surprise that they were number one in *Esquire* magazine's best contemporary fish & chip shop list.

Cod will cost you £6.90, while the more ethical coley is £5.80—choose from batter, grill or matzo meal. The chips, for an extra £1.80, are seasonal, British and double fried. Their calamari and pickled onion rings are passionately praised, as are the home-made mushy peas, tartare sauce and lemon mayonnaise. Such a delicious array of sea life and condiments means they sometimes run out of stock early: the regular evening queues are living proof of their brilliant fare. Luckily, with two shops now open the hungry mob will be appeased.

KERBISHER & MALT

FISH AND CHIPS

TAKEAWAY

AT-IN

53

KERBISHER & MALT

FAVOURITES

FISH BATTERED OR GRILLED

FISH FINGER BUTTY
CALAMARI
CHIP BUTTY
FISH NUGGETS
FISHCAKE
WHITEBAIT
FISH BITES

FRESHLY MADE SAUCES

SIDES

MUSHY PEAS
FENNEL & DILL SALAD
PICKLED ONION RINGS
K&M COLESLAW
K&M BAKED BEANS

COATS

RAFFLES CAFE DINER

Those who know about Raffles feel more secure in their nights out, for this classic establishment in the busy area of Paddington station is considered one of London's most effective hangover cures. Open till 10 pm every day, the cafe prides itself on its varied dining menu, but breakfasts here are the jewel in the crown. Generous portions and cups of filter coffee, rather than instant, contribute to Raffles' high position in the greasy spoon premier league.

The number of workers sitting in front of their breakfasts every morning should be enough proof that this is the right spot: prices are as good as you get in this part of town. Their Big Ben breakfast—announced on the window and luring tourists into this fry-up haven with a drawing of the ever-present monument—comprises two eggs, bacon, a sausage, beans, tomatoes, mushrooms and toast for the very attractive sum of £3.50.

Its rather bar-like appearance might be a bit confusing, but this is no ordinary cafe: ever since it opened about 30 years ago, manager Abdul comments, Raffles has been a popular film location. Displayed at the back are all the Hollywood and music stars that have been involved with Raffles in some way. David Bowie, Orson Welles, Fred Astaire, Laurel & Hardy and dozens more observe from the wall as you eat your chips.

Address

13 Craven Road
Paddington
W2 3BP

Telephone

020 7723 3159

GLOSSARY

Bap

Slang for bread roll, Brits often enjoy a 'Bacon Bap' or less commonly a 'Sausage Bap' for their breakfast. The most common bap consists of layers of fried bacon between a thick roll of white bread. The bacon is often smothered in a sauce, usually ketchup or brown.

Black Pudding

Not quite a pudding, this 'delicacy' is a wonderful concoction of pig's blood and oatmeal in the form of a sausage. This is often a component of the Full English Breakfast, so don't be alarmed if you think your sausage is burned, it is probably just Black Pudding.

Brew

This is a term for a cup of tea. Walk into any British cafe asking for a 'brew' you can expect a refreshing mug of tea and milk.

Bubble (Bubble and Squeak)

The stodgy English dish traditionally made with the leftover vegetables from a roast dinner. The main ingredients are potato and cabbage, which are chopped and fried in a pan together. This is not only an effective way to recycle food but it tastes great as part of a Full English Breakfast.

Builder's Tea

Colloquial term for a cheap and strong form of English Breakfast Tea. Normally builder's tea is made from one of the more common brands of tea bag such as PG Tips or Tetley. Builder's tea is most often enjoyed in a mug with milk and sugar.

Caff

Taken from the cockney pronunciation of café, the term 'caff' is used to describe a particular type of cafe seen across Britain. Caffs typically serve fried dishes, the most famous of which is the Full English Breakfast.

Chippy

This is slang for a fish & chip shop that serves the popular takeaway dish of battered fish, deep-fried and served with chunky chips. However do not be fooled by the name, 'chippies' also often serve sausages, chicken and pies.

Full English

This hearty breakfast dish usually consists of fried bacon, sausages, poached or fried egg, baked beans, grilled or fried tomatoes and toast and variations thereof. A Full English Breakfast is commonly known as a hangover cure.

Greasy Spoon

A term that describes a small and cheap cafe, sometimes dingy, but one can always expect to leave with a full stomach. These cafes serve mainly fried food and are synonymous with a location for a Full English Breakfast.

Mash

This refers to mashed potato, simply potato mashed into a paste with butter and milk. This is an essential part of the British favourite 'sausages and mash' along with many other typically British meals.

Meat Pudding

This is a name for steak and kidney pudding, so called because it is steamed and made with suet rather than pastry. A mainstay of traditional cafes, it is sometimes available in fish & chip shops.

Mushy Peas

Do not be put off by its unappetising appearance, mushy peas is a tasty side dish often enjoyed alongside a meal of fish & chips. The soaked marrowfat peas are boiled and sugar and salt are added to create this delicious yet nutritious side dish.

Roasties

This term refers to roast potatoes, an important member of the roast dinner family. Roast potatoes in a classic cafe are best served crispy with a generous helping of gravy, usually with the roasted meat of the day—beef, lamb or pork.

Wally

A 'wally' is a word to describe a gherkin, a salty and sour snack made by pickling a cucumber. A 'wally' can be enjoyed in a sandwich or, more typically, with fish & chips, simply eaten straight from the jar.

AUTHOR BIOGRAPHY

Simon Majumdar is the author of two bestselling food and travel memoirs, *Eat My Globe*, 2009 and *Eating For Britain*, 2010. He is currently working on his latest book project, *Fed, White & Blue*, which will catalogue his journey towards American citizenship through its people and its regional cuisine. Simon has written for numerous magazines, newspapers and websites, including *The Guardian*, *The Times*, *The Daily Beast* and *Rachel Ray Magazine*. He is also one of the three recurring judges on Season Five of the hit Food Network show *The Next Iron Chef* and has also become a regular on many other Food Network shows including *The Best Thing I Ever Ate*, *Extreme Chef* and *Iron Chef America*. In Autumn 2012, Simon will star in his own Food Network show, *Undercover Critics*.

THANKS

First and foremost at Black Dog Publishing thanks must go to Leonardo Collina, whose great design and beautiful photography have made the book what it is. Editorially, many thanks to Arrate Hidalgo and Thomas Howells for all their help with researching and writing. A huge thanks must also go to all the cafe and fish & chip shop owners and managers who so kindly let us into their premises, allowed us to photograph and shared some of their stories and family histories with us.

CREDITS

Unless otherwise stated all original images Leonardo Collina; p. 58, 59 all images courtesy George and Sergio at Toffs; p. 64, 65 all images courtesy Brady's and © Brian Galloway Photography; p. 158, 159 all images courtesy Concept Venues and © Tricia de Courcy Ling; pp. 166–170 all images courtesy Kerbisher & Malt and © Tom Bowles.

Black Dog Publishing Limited
10A Acton Street
London
WC1X 9NG
UK

t.   +44 (0)207 713 5097
f.   +44 (0)207 713 8682
e.   info@blackdogonline.com
www.blackdogonline.com

Edited at Black Dog Publishing by Phoebe Stubbs.
Designed at Black Dog Publishing by Leonardo Collina.

ISBN 978 1 907317 699

The information contained in this book was correct at the time of publication
but may be subject to change.

Black Dog Publishing is an environmentally responsible company.
A Guide to London's Classic Cafes and Fish & Chip Shops is printed
on sustainably sourced paper.

Also available:
Meat London: An Insider's Guide ISBN 978 1 907317 88 0
Tea & Cake London ISBN 978 1 907317 48 4

art design fashion
history photography
theory and things

www.blackdogonline.com